# CRAFTY
## IDEAS IN THE
# KITCHEN

Published in Great Britain in 1993 by
**Exley Publications Ltd, 16 Chalk Hill,**
**Watford, Herts WD1 4BN, United Kingdom.**

Published in the USA in 1993 by
**Exley Giftbooks, 359 East Main Street,**
**Suite 3D, Mount Kisco, NY 10549, USA.**

Text copyright © Myrna Daitz
Illustrations copyright © Gillian Chapman

A copy of the CIP is available from the
British Library

**ISBN 1-85015-394-9**

Series designer: Gillian Chapman.
Editorial: Margaret Montgomery.
Typeset by Brush Off Studios, St Albans, Herts AL3 4PH.
Printed and bound by Graficas Reunidas SA, Madrid, Spain.

# CRAFTY
## IDEAS IN THE
# KITCHEN

## Myrna Daitz

Pictures
by
Gillian Chapman

MT. KISCO, NEW YORK • WATFORD, UK

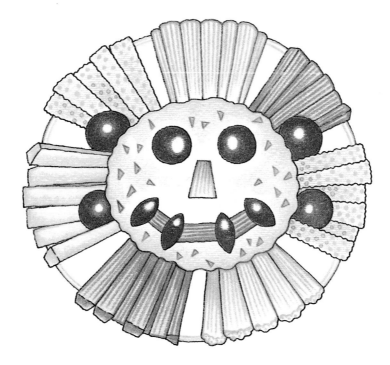

*In the same series:*

**Crafty Ideas from Junk**
**Crafty Ideas from Nature**
**Crafty Ideas for Parties**
**Crafty Ideas for Presents**
**Crafty Ideas from Science**

# Contents

# Introduction

*Crafty Ideas in the Kitchen* contains over thirty projects that can be made by children between five and ten years of age.

There are instructions for growing trees from pips and stones, making gingerbread men, date surprises and bird's nest cakes, creating a picture from different pasta shapes, turning an egg box into chicks and butterflies and printing with a potato. The projects are illustrated with step-by-step instructions and those that need adult supervision are clearly marked.

The author, Myrna Daitz, is a schoolteacher with years of experience of craft teaching. She has deliberately designed the projects to be simple and has tested them all in the classroom.

Although the projects are fun to do, they have educational value, too. Children will learn basic craft skills, like using scissors and learning to measure and fit things together, as well as developing concentration. They will also learn to use their initiative and work things out for themselves.

Children shouldn't worry if their completed projects don't look like the ones in the book. It is important that they feel free to be creative and have a sense of achievement. As most of the materials needed for the projects will be readily available in the home or school, there's no great expense involved if the first attempt doesn't turn out quite right and has to be discarded.

So, have fun and enjoy yourselves!

# Potato Printing

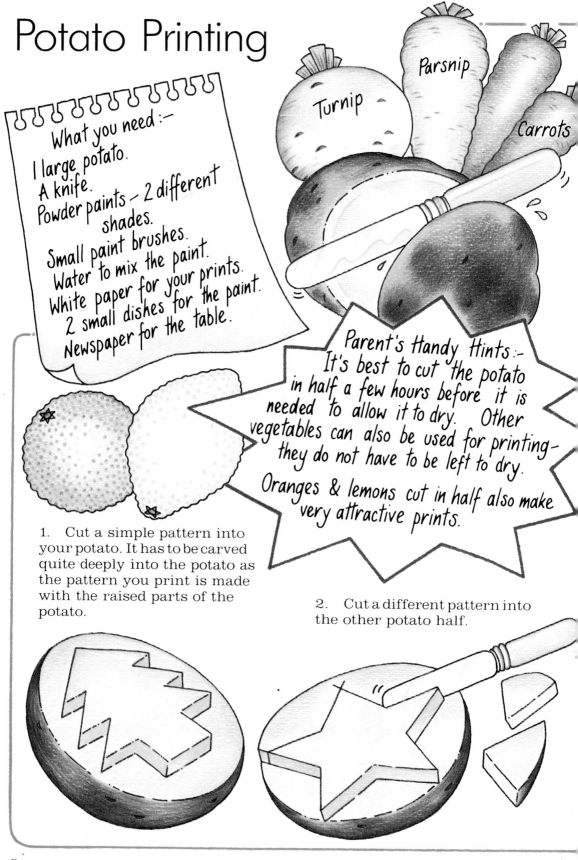

**What you need :-**

1 large potato.
A knife.
Powder paints – 2 different shades.
Small paint brushes.
Water to mix the paint.
White paper for your prints.
2 small dishes for the paint.
Newspaper for the table.

Turnip

Parsnip

Carrots

**Parent's Handy Hints :-**
It's best to cut the potato in half a few hours before it is needed to allow it to dry. Other vegetables can also be used for printing – they do not have to be left to dry.

Oranges & lemons cut in half also make very attractive prints.

1.   Cut a simple pattern into your potato. It has to be carved quite deeply into the potato as the pattern you print is made with the raised parts of the potato.

2.   Cut a different pattern into the other potato half.

3.   Mix the paints to a thick consistency. Using the paintbrush, paint the potato blocks.

4.   Press the potatoes down well on your sheet of white paper. When you have got used to printing in this way, you can start making up interesting designs.
You can print this way on an old tee shirt, but do get permission first.

# Seed and Sow

**What you need:—**
Several large glass jars.
Absorbent paper.
Water.
Bean, pea and radish seeds.

**Parent's Handy Hints:—**
This is a good project for small children as they can actually watch the seeds growing. Bean sprouts also grow well and are fun to eat. Peanuts grow quickly, but plant the nuts in compost.

1. Line a large jar with absorbent paper and pour in 150ml (5 fl.oz.) water, slightly dampening the paper as you pour the water in.

2. Put the seeds in between the paper and the glass, allowing the paper to hold the seeds. Put three or four of the same kind of seeds in each jar.

3. Keep the jars in a light, warm place and sprinkle with water when the paper feels dry.

4. When your seeds have grown very strong roots, they can be planted out in the spring or summer.

150 ml. 5 fl.oz.

Peas

Beans

# Trees From Pips and Stones

**What you need :-**
Several small plant pots
— with saucers.
The same number of clean
jam jars.
Special seed compost.
Pips - from oranges, lemons,
grapefruit or tangerines. Stones—
peach, date, cherry or apricot.

1.    Fill the plant pots with the compost and push two pips OR one stone into the compost until they are covered.

2.    Sprinkle with enough water to dampen the compost, then cover each plant pot with an upturned jam jar. This makes a miniature greenhouse.

orange pips    peach stone

3.    Leave the pots in a warm, dark place until the pip or stone begins to sprout. Check from time to time that the compost is moist, as the seed could take some weeks to germinate.

4.    When the pip or stone begins to sprout, remove the jam jar and put the pot into a light, airy place.

**Parent's Handy Hints :-**
Help your child to label and date each plant.
Special seed compost is available at gardening shops.
Make sure your child does not over-water the plants.

peach    orange    date    cherry

11

# Mottled Eggs

Parent's Handy Hint:—
This only works on white eggs, as the eggs will turn yellow and brown.

**What you need :—**
An egg, boiled for 20 mins. (and cooled.)
A large, dark skinned onion.
String.
A small piece of muslin.
A saucepan.          Knife.
Cold water.
Spoon.

Help will be needed to peel the onion.

1.  Peel the dark skin from the onion. Slightly dampen the skin with warm water.

2.  Wrap the egg firmly in the onion skin, using up all the skin. Wrap the egg in the small piece of muslin and tie it tightly with the string.

3.  Place the egg in the pan, cover with cold water and bring the water slowly to the boil. Turn the heat down very low, and let the water simmer for 25 minutes. Be sure there is enough water in the pan to completely cover the egg and keep checking to see that it has not boiled away.

4.  Remove the egg with a spoon, and leave to cool. Then remove the string, muslin and onion skin. You will now have a mottled golden yellow and brown egg.

# Egg Shell Mosaic

1.  Cut the cardboard to the size you require for your picture. Carefully put adhesive tape around the edge of the cardboard to make an attractive border for your mosaic.

2.  Plan your design on a piece of paper, and then very carefully draw it on your cardboard. A large bold picture is very attractive.

3.  Leave your egg shells in as large pieces as possible to paint. Then when dry, break into small pieces for your mosaic.

What you need :—
The broken up shells of 6 eggs.
A piece of stiff cardboard.
Bright adhesive tape.
An adhesive picture hook.
Wallpaper paste.
A glue brush.      Scissors.
Drawing paper.      Pencil.
Poster paints and paint brush.

Parent's Handy Hints :—
Whenever you use eggs, wash and dry the discarded shells, and use for craft work. If clean & dry the shells will keep indefinitely.

4.  Make a fairly thick mixture of wallpaper paste, and brush it carefully over your design. Gently place the fragments of egg shell on to the pasted surface.

5.  When the picture is completely dry, secure the picture hook to the back.

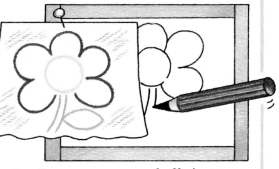

# A Potato Shoot

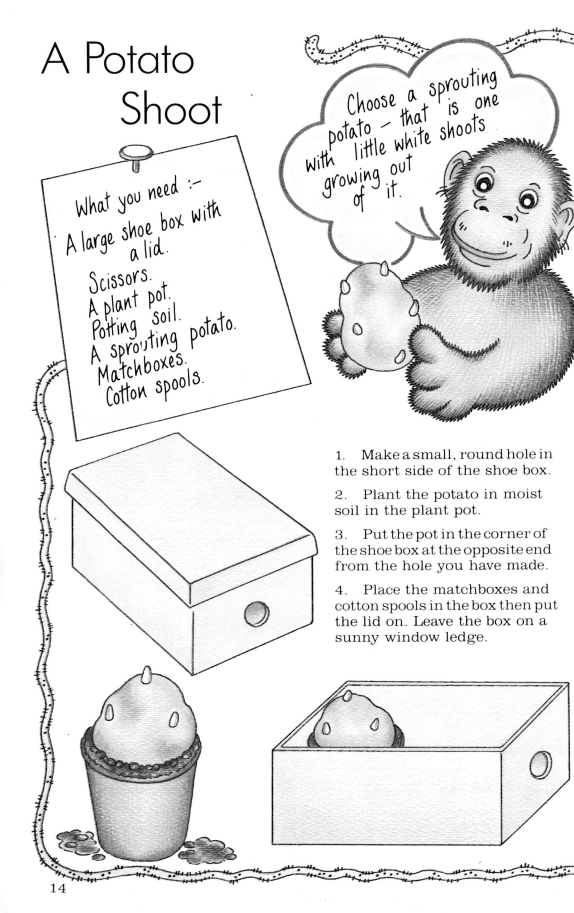

Choose a sprouting potato — that is one with little white shoots growing out of it.

What you need :-
A large shoe box with a lid.
Scissors.
A plant pot.
Potting soil.
A sprouting potato.
Matchboxes.
Cotton spools.

1. Make a small, round hole in the short side of the shoe box.

2. Plant the potato in moist soil in the plant pot.

3. Put the pot in the corner of the shoe box at the opposite end from the hole you have made.

4. Place the matchboxes and cotton spools in the box then put the lid on. Leave the box on a sunny window ledge.

5. Open the box after three days and you will see that the shoot has found its way over the "obstacles" you left in its way and has reached the hole.

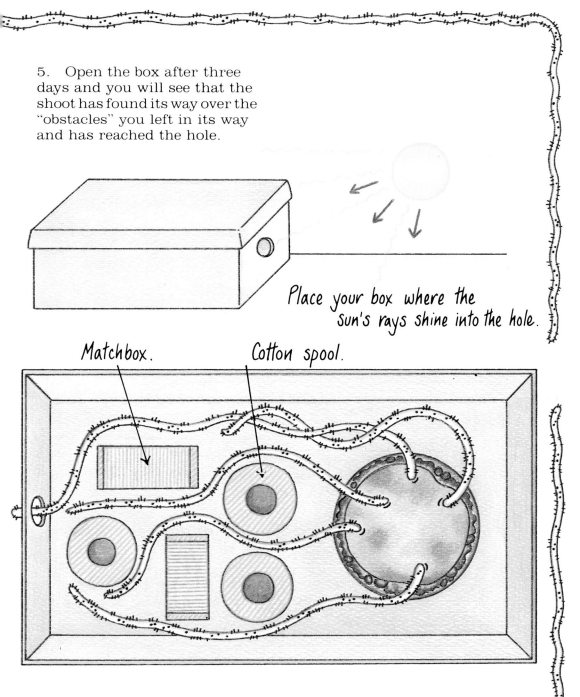

Place your box where the sun's rays shine into the hole.

Matchbox.

Cotton spool.

## SCIENCE FACTS

*Plants have LIGHT-SENSITIVE CELLS that show the plant which direction to grow in. The tiny amount of light entering your shoe box made the shoot twist and bend until it reached the light.*

*The shoot will be white, not green as it should be, because the CHLOROPHYLL, which makes it green, cannot be made in the dark.*

# Dry Water

What you need :-
Ice cube trays.
Diluted orange juice.
A freezer compartment
of a refrigerator.

Science Fact :-
Water can be WET
or DRY !

1. Pour the diluted orange juice into the cube trays.

2. Place the cube trays into the freezer compartment of a refrigerator.

3. When solid, dip the trays quickly into hot water to release the cubes then – ENJOY.

**SCIENCE FACTS**

*Water can be WET or DRY. LIQUID water is wet. Water is not always liquid. A delicious ice cube is water that has been frozen into ICE.*

# Sugar Crystals

### What you need :-

A drinking glass.
Water.
Sugar.
A small pan.
A pencil.
Cotton thread.
A paper clip.     A cup.

1.   WITH THE SUPERVISION OF AN ADULT put three-quarters of a glass of water into a small pan. Bring it to the boil then ask the adult to remove the pan from the heat and put it on a heatproof surface.

2.   Stir three cups of sugar into the water, little by little, until no more will dissolve.

3.   Carefully pour this mixture into the glass.

4.   Tie a short length of thread around the middle of the pencil. Attach a paper clip to the bottom of the thread to act as a weight, then lay the pencil across the top of the glass and adjust the thread until it almost reaches the bottom of the glass.

5.   Put the glass into a warm place for a day or two.

## SCIENCE FACTS

*Soon you will find that the thread is covered with CRYSTALS of sugar. As the solution that you made cooled, it could no longer keep all its sugar and had to give some of it up in the form of crystals.*

Science Fact :-
These crystals are of the same shape as the sugar crystals you started with — - but they are much LARGER!

17

# Invisible Ink

1. Cut the lemon in half and squeeze out the juice.

2. Put the lemon juice into a cup.

3. Clean the nib of the mapping pen, then dip it into the lemon juice and write your letter on the white paper.

4. When the paper is dry, it will look completely blank.

5. Very carefully hold the paper in front of a radiator to warm it. You will soon see your letter appear.

## SCIENCE FACTS

*The lemon juice has a LOWER COMBUSTION POINT (burning) than the paper and as the paper warms slightly, you will see your writing gradually appear. It will look pale brown.*

*This is a fun way to send secret messages to your friends. You must tell them the secret of the radiator first.*

What you need :-

A cup.
A large lemon.
A mapping pen.
White paper.

Remember –
You must tell your friends the secret of the radiator first !

# Magic Water

1.  Cut up the red cabbage and soak it in the bowl of very hot water for at least an hour. You now have violet water.

2.  Strain the liquid into a drinking glass.

3.  Place the three wine glasses on a table. Into the first glass put plain water. Into the second glass, put white vinegar. In the third glass put water with baking soda mixed in it.

4.  Pour a little of the violet water into each glass.

What you need :-

A piece of red cabbage.
A small bowl of very hot water.
3 wine glasses.
A drinking glass.
White vinegar.
2 teaspoons of baking soda.
A small strainer.

plain water

white vinegar

baking soda sol.

**SCIENCE FACTS**

*The PLAIN WATER will remain violet.*
*The WHITE VINEGAR will turn red.*
*The BAKING SODA solution will turn green.*

*The violet cabbage dye has the property of turning red in ACID liquids (the vinegar) and green in ALKALINE liquids (baking soda). It doesn't change in the NEUTRAL water.*

*Scientists can find out whether a liquid is ACID or ALKALINE by using similar detecting liquids. These are called INDICATORS.*

# Making Starch

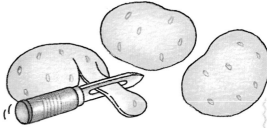

What you need :-

3 large potatoes.
A potato peeler.
A grater.
A large clean handkerchief.
A small mixing bowl.
Water.

1. Peel and then grate the three potatoes.

2. Half fill the bowl with water.

3. Put the grated potato into the handkerchief. Dip the handkerchief into the water and then squeeze it very hard into the bowl. Keep dipping the handkerchief into the water and squeezing it out after each dipping. The water will become very cloudy. Leave the water to stand for an hour.

4. After an hour, a white powder will have settled at the bottom of the bowl. Carefully pour off as much of the clear water ABOVE the powder as possible. Leave the powder for a couple of hours to dry out.

## SCIENCE FACTS

*The powder you have produced is STARCH. Starch is a very useful material. Potatoes, rice, barley, rye and wheat contain large amounts of starch. When you eat foods high in starch, chemicals that are present in the digestive juices change the starch to sugars that can be used up by the body.*

*STARCH is put on cloth to give it weight and smoothness. The household starch that you have made can be used on clothes to make them smooth when they are ironed.*

# How Do Plants Drink?

**What you need :-**
A glass jar or bottle.
Water.
Food dye.
A celery stick.
A knife.

1. Half fill the jar with water and add a teaspoon of food dye.

2. Cut a small piece off the end of the celery. Stand it in the jar of water and leave it in a warm, light place for a day.

3. Remove the celery from the water, wash it and then slice off about 4cm (1½").

**Science Fact :-** You can see where the plant has taken up the dyed water.

**SCIENCE FACTS**

*When you examine the cut you will see dots where the stem has taken up the dyed water. It will be like this all the way up the celery stick. All plants need water to stay alive and to make them grow.*

# Melon Seed Necklace

1. Wash and thoroughly dry the melon seeds.

2. Cut the button thread to the size you need for your necklace. Tie a knot at one end of the thread.

**What you need :-**
Melon seeds.
Strong white button thread.
A darning needle.
Poster paints & brush
Newspapers.    Scissors.

3. Thread the darning needle and very carefully push the needle and thread through each melon seed. String the seeds in this way until the whole length of thread is almost full. Tie the end of the thread to the knot you started with.

4. Spread out the finished necklace on a sheet of newspaper and very carefully paint the seeds. Remove the necklace from the newspaper and hang up to dry. Repeat the painting process on the back of the seeds. Hang up to dry.

**Parent's Handy Hints :-**
Make sure you put down plenty of newspaper before your child starts painting!

# Shell Boats

## What you need :–

Walnuts.
Nut crackers. *
Model clay.
Paper.
Toothpicks.

* try to save as many unbroken shell halves as you can!

**Parent's Handy Hint :–**
Encourage your child to eat nuts – they are far healthier than chocolates.

1.   Very carefully crack a walnut. If you prise the two halves gently apart, one half will be unbroken. Use this for your boat.

2.   Put a small piece of model clay in the shell.

3.   Make sails from the paper.

4.   To make the masts, put a toothpick in, out and through the sail.

5.   Push the masts and sails into the model clay.

# A Cook's Herb Garden

**What you need :-**
Several yogurt pots.
Compost.      A bowl.
Packets of herb seeds.
Ice lolly sticks.
A felt tipped pen.
A small tray.
A sharp pencil.
Model clay.
Cellophane.
Oil based paints & brush.

MODEL CLAY →

**Parent's Handy Hint :-**
This makes a useful present for a person who enjoys the cooking and will use the freshly grown herbs.

1. Decorate the yogurt pots with bright paint.

2. Carefully make several drainage holes at the bottom of each pot using the skewer.

3. Put the compost into a large bowl. Water it well. Take out a handful and squeeze the moisture out of it. Gently press it into the pot. Continue until all the pots are full.

4. Sprinkle the herbs into each pot and press them gently into the compost.

5. Write the name of each herb on an ice lolly stick then press the correct stick into each pot of herbs.

6. Put all the cartons on to the tray and cover it with cellophane.

PARSLEY

PARSLEY

THYME

SAGE

# Bumpy Dough Pictures

What you need :-
A large piece of cardboard.
Wide sticky tape.
3/4 cup of flour.
1/4 cup of salt.
Water.      A wooden spoon.
Powder paint.
Several bowls - one for each dough mixture.
A large mixing bowl.

1. Mix the flour and salt with a few spoonfuls of water. Mix very well and keep adding water slowly until the mixture is a soft dough.

2. Share the dough out between your small bowls.

3. Put a spoonful of paint in each bowl and mix gently into the dough until you have several bright doughs.

4. Using a pencil, draw the picture you want on the cardboard.

5. Now start building up your picture, using the different doughs.

To finish the picture press the sticky tape all around the edge of the picture to make a border.

# Egg Box Chicks

1.  Take two polystyrene egg boxes. Carefully remove the fastening flap (keep to use later) and cut the lid in half longways. Staple the front three egg sections securely to the base.

2.  Cut out beaks and feet from pieces of bright cardboard using the patterns shown here as a guide. Fold the beak in half.

What you need :-
2 polystyrene egg boxes.
Scissors.
Stapler.
Cardboard.
Plastic based glue.
Darning needle.
Feathers.

3.  Make a small slit in the front of each egg section and insert the beaks.

4.  Draw on eyes using a felt-tipped pen and glue the feet into place using a plastic-based glue.

5.  Cut out the small raised pieces from the fastening flap and glue on to the chicks' heads. Using a darning needle pierce a hole in the back of each chick's head and insert a bright feather for the tail.

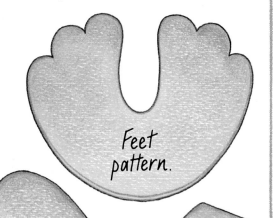

Feet pattern.

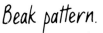

Beak pattern.

# Egg Box Butterfly

1. Take a cardboard egg box and cut off the lid.

2. Cut the base in half longways to give three egg sections and paint these brightly.

3. Cut out a pair of wings from thin cardboard in the shape shown and paint or crayon them in a pattern of your choice.

What you need:-
A cardboard egg box.
Scissors.
Paint or crayons.
Thin cardboard.
Adhesive tape.
A pipe cleaner.
Felt tipped pens.

Wing pattern.

4. Make a slit on either side of the middle egg section and gently push through the narrow end of the wings. Bend down the ends inside and secure with adhesive tape.

5. Make two small holes in the first egg section. Take a pipe cleaner and cut in half. Push half through one hole and out through the other to make antennae. Finish by drawing on a face with felt-tipped pen.

Parent's Handy Hints :-
Help the child to make the "wing" slits with the scissors.

# Little Nut Tree

1. Cover the plant pot with the paper, and secure with adhesive tape.

What you need:-
A 15cm. (6") plant pot.
Wrapping paper.
Adhesive tape.
A selection of nuts and raisins. Model clay.
Small fir cones.
An interesting branch with twigs.
A needle and thread.

2. Put a large piece of model clay inside the pot, pressing it firmly to the base and making sure it is in the middle.

3. Press the branch into the model clay to make it stand firmly, then fill the pot up to the top with soil.

4. Wrap nuts and raisins in the paper.

5. Thread the needle. Carefully push the needle and thread through the paper wrapping of the nuts and raisins. Tie lengths of thread around the top of each small fir cone, leaving a loop at the top, and then hang them all from the twigs.

Parent's Handy Hints :-
This makes a delightful table decoration for a party.
Small messages can be slipped inside the wrappings with the nuts and sweets!

# A Festive Candle

Parent's Handy Hint :-
Supervise slicing the base off the orange - juice must not be allowed to escape.

**What you need :-**
A large orange.
1 birthday cake candle and 1 birthday cake candle holder.
A small piece of gold tinsel.
Toothpicks.  A knife.
A saucer.
Candied fruit, nuts and raisins.

1.  Slice a piece from the bottom of the orange so that it will stand in the saucer and not roll over.

2.  Press the candle holder into the top of the orange and put the candle in. Put a ring of tinsel round the holder.

3.  Press the toothpicks all around the orange and put a small piece of candied fruit on each one.

4.  Put the orange on a saucer and fill the saucer with nuts and raisins.

# Pasta Polly Parrot

What you need:-
I piece of thick white cardboard, approx. 30 x 25 cms. (12" x 10")
Small packet of wall paper paste.
Paste brush.
Light shade of powder paint.
A piece of bright foil.
Scissors.    Ruler.
2 stick-on picture hooks.
Piece of white paper - same size as cardboard.

Water melon seeds, washed and well dried on absorbent paper.
Dried lentils, split peas and different types of beans. (these are called PULSES).
Pasta shapes - spaghetti and macaroni.
Rice (white & brown).
Pieces of crushed egg shell.

1.  Draw your parrot and arrange the seeds, pulses, pasta, rice and crushed egg shells on the piece of white paper. Keep moving them around until you choose a design that looks really good.

25cm.(10")
2cm. (¾")
30 cm. (12")

2.  Cut the bright foil into long strips approximately 2cm (¾") wide, to fit all around the edges of the cardboard.

3.  Using half the packet of wallpaper paste, make the mixture up until it is quite thick.

4. Add 2 teaspoonfuls of the powder paint, and mix well until it has blended in.

5. Spread the paste all over the cardboard.

6. Stick the foil around the edges of the picture to make a very attractive frame.

7. Following your own design, place your seeds, pulses, rice and crushed egg shells on to the glued surface of the cardboard. Complete one area at a time, pressing gently onto the paste.

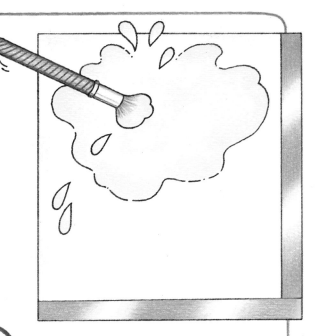

8. Leave to dry for a couple of days.

9. Attach two picture hooks to the back of your collage, using either adhesive tape or glue.

Parent's Handy Hints :—
Bright foil is more interesting to use than paper. Use recycled foil if possible.

Stick-on picture hooks can be bought in most hardware shops.

Water melon seeds keep well when washed and dried thoroughly.

Egg shell should be washed, dried and crushed in between paper.

# Bird's Nest Cakes

These Bird's Nests are just right for parties!

**What you need:—**
8 paper cake cases.
½ coconut (removed from shell).
200g. (7oz.) cooking chocolate.
A saucepan half-filled with hot water.
50g. (2oz.) ground almonds.
50g. (2oz.) confectioner's/icing sugar.
1 teaspoon lemon juice.
25g. (1oz.) raisins.
1 egg yolk. A wooden spoon.
A grater. A knife.
Heatproof dish.

**Parent's Handy Hint:—** Supervision of the melting of the chocolate is advised.

1.  Grate the coconut. Put the heatproof dish over the pan of simmering water, break the chocolate into small pieces and let it melt in the dish over the water.

2.  When all the chocolate has melted, carefully remove the heatproof dish and using the wooden spoon and the knife spread a thick layer of chocolate in each cake case following the complete shape of the bottom and sides. Let this set for about 10 minutes then give the cake cases a second coating (you may have to put the chocolate in the dish back on the pan of hot water). Put the chocolate coated cases in a cool place to set, then gently peel away the paper leaving a chocolate case.

3.  Mix the grated coconut and raisins with the rest of the melted chocolate and fill the chocolate "nests" with the mixture.

4.  To make the bird's eggs: Put the almonds, icing sugar, lemon juice and egg yolk in a bowl and knead together well. Shape into eggs, roll in icing sugar and place the "eggs" in the "nests".

# Fresh Lemonade

Supervise boiling the water.

**What you need :—**
3 fresh lemons.
1·5 litres (60 fl.oz.) of cold water.
2 tablespoons of brown sugar.
1 saucepan.
A potato peeler.

A lemon squeezer.
A strainer.
A knife.
A long handled wooden spoon.
A large heat proof bowl.

**Parent's Handy Hint :—**
Show your child how to use the potato peeler, as this will remove the lemon rind not the pith.

1.  Thoroughly rinse and dry the lemons, and peel them very thinly using the potato peeler.

2.  Put 250ml (10 fl.oz.) of cold water into the saucepan, add the sugar and the lemon rind and stir well. Bring the mixture slowly to the boil and simmer for 10 minutes, stirring occasionally with a long-handled wooden spoon.

3.  Cut the lemons in half, squeeze out the juice into a large bowl, add the rest of the cold water to the lemon juice in the bowl and then very carefully add the hot liquid from the pan and stir well.

4.  When the lemonade is cold, carefully pour it through the strainer into a jug. Add ice cubes and serve.

# Chocolate Truffles

## What you need :-
Small paper cases.
110g. (4oz.) icing sugar (confectioner's sugar)
85g. (2½oz.) cocoa powder.
3 tablespoons of thick cream.
Chocolate vermicelli.
A large bowl.     A sieve.
          A wooden spoon.

1.   Put the sieve over the bowl and shake the sugar and cocoa into the bowl through it.

2.   Gently mix in the cream.

3.   Thoroughly dust your hands with sugar and roll the mixture into small balls.

4.   Roll each ball in chocolate vermicelli.

5.   Leave for 2 hours in the refrigerator.

6.   Put the truffles in the paper cases and put into a decorated container. DELIVER THE PRESENT IMMEDIATELY.

Adult's Handy Hint :-
If the present is for an adult, add a few drops of rum to the cream!

# Date Surprises

What you need :-

Fresh dates.
Whole skinned almonds.
Powdered cardamom
   seeds.
Marzipan.
A sharp knife.

Parent's Handy Hint :-
DO NOT let the child use
the sharp knife without
ADULT SUPERVISION.

1.  Slit the dates with a sharp-pointed knife and remove the stones.

2.  Sprinkle some cardamom powder inside the date and put in an almond. Close the date.

3.  Cut out a small square of marzipan and seal the date inside the marzipan.

These make an ideal gift for a friend or relative.

# Coconut Snowballs

**What you need :-**
55g. (2oz.) shredded coconut.
55g. (2oz.) plain biscuits (crackers).
55g. (2oz.) sultanas.
55g. (2oz.) almonds.
75g. (2½ fl. oz.) fresh cream.
A rolling pin.     A knife.
A bowl.             A spoon.
A bag.

**Parent's Handy Hint :-**
You can make snowmen by putting two coconut balls together. Use pieces of currant and cherry for the eyes & mouth.

1.   Crumble the biscuits (crackers) with a rolling-pin.

2.   Chop the nuts and the fruit into small pieces.

3.   Put the crumbs, chopped nuts and fruit into a bowl and add the cream.

4.   Mix well.

5.   Shape the mixture into small balls.

6.   Put the coconut into a bag and drop the balls in, a few at a time.

7.   Roll them about and shake them in the bag. This helps to make them rounder.

8.   When you take them out, they should be covered in coconut. They are ready to eat straightaway.

# Crispy Crispies

Supervise the melting of the chocolate!

**What you need :-**
Cornflakes or rice crispies.
Bar of chocolate.
125g. (4oz.) icing (confectioner's) sugar.
Paper cases.
1-2 tablespoons hot water.
Chopped cherry & angelica.
A bowl of hot water.
A bowl & a spoon.

1.  Put the chocolate in a bowl and place it over another bowl of hot, but *not* boiling, water until the chocolate melts.

2.  Remove the bowl with the melted chocolate and stir in the cereal, being sure it's well mixed in and all covered in chocolate.

3.  Wash your hands. Now for the messy part. With your hands, roll the crispies into small balls. Put into paper cases and leave to set.

4.  Mix the sugar and hot water together in a bowl until smooth. Put half a teaspoon on top of each crispie.

5.  Decorate the top of each crispie with a piece of cherry and two pieces of angelica.

# Monster Munch

1.  Mix the cream cheese with the apple juice to make a creamy mixture.

2.  Cut the apple into quarters and remove the core from each piece.

3.  Chop the apple and cheese into small pieces and add to the creamy mixture.

4.  Wash the vegetables and cut into sticks.

5.  Put the dip on a plate and decorate with small tomatoes, chopped nuts and vegetable sticks. Surround with the bread sticks and more vegetable sticks.

Parent's Handy Hint :- This healthy dip can be made more appealing to children by creating a MONSTER face with cut tomatoes & carrots! Help may be needed to cut the vegetables.

# Leopard Cake

**What you need :-**
1 sponge roll.
300 ml. (10 fl. oz.) whipping cream.
Chocolate drops.
Cherries.
One chocolate finger.
Yellow food dye.

**Parent's Handy Hint :-**
The sponge roll can be bought ready made. Help may be needed to whip the cream.

1. Whip the cream until it is stiff, then add a few drops of yellow food dye.

2. Put the sponge roll on a plate and spread the whipped cream all over it. Using a fork, make ridges in the cream.

3. Make a face at one end of the roll, using chocolate drops for eyes and a cherry for the nose. Put the chocolate finger at the other end for a tail, and cover the "body" in chocolate drops for spots.

# Apple Surprises

What you need :-

8 small apples.

8 lollipop sticks.

200g. (7oz.) unsweetened cooking chocolate.

100g. (3½oz.) dried banana flakes.

A saucepan half filled with boiling water.

A heatproof bowl.

A wooden spoon.

Waxed cooking paper.

Supervise the boiling and simmering of the water.

Parent's Handy Hint :- Choose apples with a long stalk on them, then these can be bent around the stick to hold the apple firmly.

1.   Wash the apples and dry on absorbent paper. Push a stick firmly into each apple and twist the stalk round the stick. Break the chocolate into small pieces and put into a heatproof bowl. Place the bowl on top of a pan of gently simmering water.

2.   When the chocolate is soft and runny, carefully remove the bowl from the saucepan and dip each apple into the chocolate. Turn the apple round and round using the stick until the apple is well covered.

3.   Lift the apple out carefully and then roll the chocolate apple in a flat dish of flaked banana chips. Stand the apples, with the stick pointing up, on the waxed paper to set. Store in a very cold place or in a refrigerator.

# Cucumber Cactus

What you need :-
A cucumber.
A selection of the following :-
olives, small white onions, raisins,
small tomatoes, grapes, cheese,
pineapple, carrots, salami,
toothpicks.
2 whole carrots.

2.    Peel and grate the carrots.

3.    Cut the cucumber into two pieces – one longer than the other. Stand the two pieces next to each other on a plate and surround with grated carrot.

4.    Carefully push the toothpicks into the cucumber pieces so they look like prickles.

1.    Thread each toothpick with two or three pieces of food of your choice. These will be the prickles for the cactus.

Adult's Handy Hint :-
The "prickles" make
healthy snacks & allow
children to experiment
with combinations of
different foods.

43

# Coconut Mice

1. Put the condensed milk, coconut and a few drops of food dye into a bowl and mix together.

2. When thoroughly mixed, take out a spoonful of mixture and, with clean fingers, form into an oval shape.

3. For the face, press one end in to make a pointed nose. Add small pieces of licorice for the eyes and mouth and thin strips for whiskers.

4. Push two almonds in for ears and add a strip of licorice for the tail.

5. Repeat steps 2, 3 and 4, until all the mixture has been used, then arrange on a plate to make a nest of coconut mice.

Adult's Handy Hints :–
Explain the importance of hygiene when handling food. Keep the mice in the refrigerator until they are needed.

# Yummy Bunnies

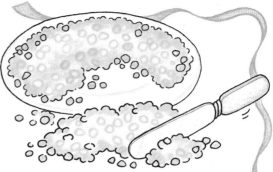

What you need :—

1 packet of green jelly.
1 can of pear halves.
Small pieces of chocolate.
Flaked almonds.
Cherries.
A little whipped cream.

Parent's Handy Hint :—

Supervise the child making the jelly with hot water.

1. Make the jelly according to the instructions on the packet and put in a refrigerator to set.

2. When the jelly has set, chop it up and arrange it on a plate for grass.

3. Drain the pear halves and place them in the "grass".

4. On each pear half put two pieces of chocolate for eyes, a cherry for the nose and two almonds for ears. Add a blob of whipped cream for the bunny's fluffy tail!

# Gingerbread Men

1. Trace our picture of a gingerbread man then transfer it to a piece of thick cardboard and cut it out.

2. In a pan, heat the margarine with the golden syrup and the sugar. Do not allow to boil.

3. Dissolve the bicarbonate of soda in a little water and add this to the syrup mixture. Stir gently with the wooden spoon.

**What you need :-**
85g. (3½ oz.) margarine.
2 tablespoons of Golden Syrup.
57g. (2oz.) sugar.
½ teaspoon of bicarbonate of soda.
200g. (8oz.) flour.
1½ teaspoons of ground ginger.
Currants or raisins.
A long handled wooden spoon.
A sieve.  A rolling pin.

4. Remove the pan from the stove and place on a heat-proof surface.

Parent's Handy Hints :-
Talk to your child about SAFETY in the KITCHEN.
The melting of the syrup & sugar, and the use of the oven MUST BE SUPERVISED.

5. Put the sieve over the pan and gently add the flour and ground ginger, shaking them through the sieve. Mix well to make a firm dough. Put the mixture in a clean, dry bowl and cover with a tea cloth. Leave for one hour.

6. Roll out the dough then make the gingerbread men by gently placing your shape on the dough and cutting around it. Use the currants for eyes and nose.

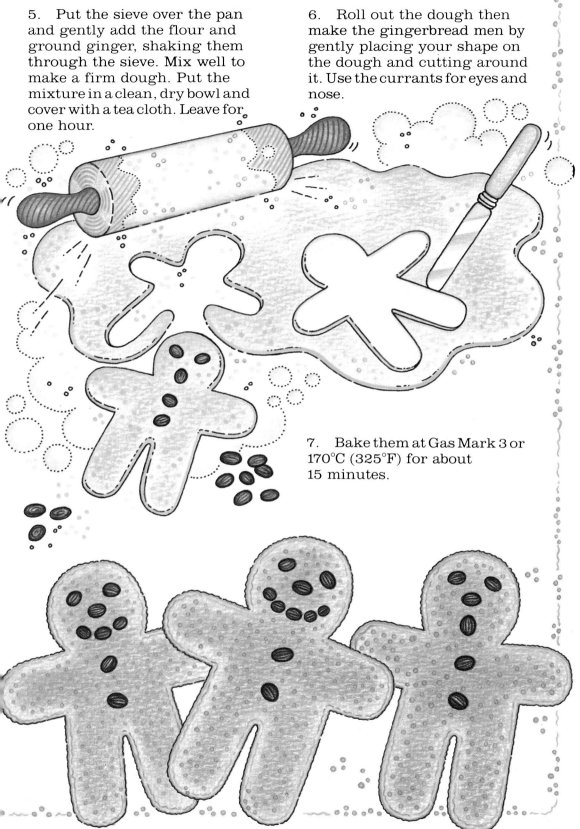

7. Bake them at Gas Mark 3 or 170°C (325°F) for about 15 minutes.